Praise for *I Wish My Father*

"What poetry teaches us most importantly is how to be human: its purpose is ontological; its affect, sacramental. Leslea Newman's *I Wish My Father* is comprised of narrative poems about her father in the last years of his life, and retrospectively, throughout his ninety-plus years. Her wisely distilled and carefully rendered details are paired with his habits of speech so they succeed in embodying his way of being in the world. We see this man in relation to those he loved, those he served, those he interacted with from the casually flirtatious to profoundly and grandly loving, and we learn how he comported himself as a person. And while these poems are personal, they are transpersonal as well: an entire world, a time, a place, a culture...came into this world and has left it. How to express the meaning of all that? Newman's poems succeed in making the best possible approximation: With precision, compression, a graceful style earned through a lifetime of writing, paired with Newman's tender and compassionate gaze, we are given the true good, the enduring image of the person kept beyond time, love's greatest blessing. There is so much more than delight and recognition encountered in reading the poems in this collection. They comprise an act of honoring that witnessed, enriches the reader, and that honors, by the very fact of their being, the reader's experience. Who could ask more of a work of art?" —**Gray Jacobik** author of *Eleanor* and *The Banquet: New and Selected Poems*

Poetry Collections by Lesléa Newman

Lovely

I Carry My Mother

October Mourning: A Song for Matthew Shepard
(novel-in-verse)

I Remember: Hachiko Speaks
(chapbook)

Nobody's Mother

Signs of Love

Still Life With Buddy

The Little Butch Book

I Wish My Father

I Wish My Father

Lesléa Newman

HEADMISTRESS PRESS

ISBN 9781733534567

Cover art © 2014 Carol Marine.
Blue Tie Man, 7x5in., oil on panel, carolmarine.com
Cover & book design by Mary Meriam.

PUBLISHER
Headmistress Press
60 Shipview Lane
Sequim, WA 98382
Telephone: 917-428-8312
Email: headmistresspress@gmail.com
Website: headmistresspress.blogspot.com

for my father, Edward Newman

March 15, 1927 – December 12, 2017

may his memory be for a blessing

Contents

*Science tells us that to live
One needs air and water,
But to have a better life
One must have a daughter.*

*To have one so talented, caring, and bright,
Even makes old age all right.*

—poem written by my father
for my 60th birthday

WHEN MY FATHER WAKES UP

on that first sweltering night
of that first scalding summer
soaked in sweat like my mother

when she suffered those terrible
hot flashes 40 years ago,
he stumbles out of bed

and lumbers to the archaic air
conditioner, fumbling for the right
button to bring it back to life

with a wheeze and a groan and
a thump. Next he shuffles across
the faded carpet, slides between

the worn sheets, and lifts the torn
blanket to cover my mother
who will surely grow stiff

from the frigid air blowing
between them as she had
for more than 60 years.

Who could blame him
for forgetting she had left
him and was now slumbering

on the other side of town
wrapped in a shroud beneath
the stony, stubborn ground?

How he missed
her old cold
shoulder

DO YOU THINK YOUR FATHER

would take me to the theatre?"
A woman pulls me aside,
her pointed red nails digging

into the doughy flesh of my bare
upper arm. It is a hot August
afternoon, made hotter still

by the heat of the oven
which I have just opened
to take out a pan of kugel

a neighbor brought by and needed
to be warmed. How did I wind up
alone in the kitchen with this

woman who does not look unlike
my mother? Styled and stiff
thinning brown hair dried out

from too many years of dyeing,
lipstick two shades too dark,
forehead lined like notebook paper

hope springing eternal
in her made-up myopic eyes.
I drop the metal pan of food

on the counter with a clatter,
open a drawer near the sink
and lift my mother's gleaming

kitchen knife. What is this woman's
name? Edna, Edith, Estelle,
Esther! A woman my mother used

to play canasta with and never
particularly liked. "She cheats,"
my mother told me on a scorching

afternoon not that long ago.
"She picks out all the cashews
in the bridge mix. And she has eyes

for your father." I cut the kugel
into even, sharp-edged squares
missing my even sharper-edged mother

who would curl her lip and shoot
me a silent "I told you so" look
to hear Esther ask me if my father

would take her to the theatre
the very afternoon after
the morning of my mother's funeral.

YES WE HAVE NO

bananas." My father croons
off key as we stroll
through the supermarket.

"Shall we get some?" he asks,
a standing joke between us.
My father hates bananas,

peaches, plums, mangoes
anything mushy makes him
shudder in disgust.

"Remember that time
I baked you banana bread?"
I stop our cart to ask.

"You loved it until I told you
what it was, remember?"
"Really?" my father says.

"Impossible." He backs away
from the bananas as though
they mean him harm.

"I don't remember."
"Sure you do," I insist.
"I put three pieces on a plate

and you ate them all.
It was the summer before
I went off to college."

My father steers clear
of the bananas and pushes
the cart towards the deli.

"Where'd you go to college again?"
he asks, placing a package
of rugelach into the cart.

"Vermont," I say, removing
the rugelach which is bad
for his diabetes. "Don't you

remember? We drove up
and stopped for lunch
at that diner in Montpelier,

and the one woman working
there was seating people,
taking orders, cooking,

running the register
and Mom felt so sorry
for her, she offered

to leap over the counter
and lend a hand, remember?"
At this my father brightens.

"Ah, your mother," he says.
"She could have done it.
She could do anything."

"Almost anything," I correct him.
"There was one thing
she could never do."

I reach for a bag of whole
wheat bagels. "What's that?"
my father asks, genuinely curious.

"She could never get you
to eat a banana."
"That's true." My father's chortle

dies in his throat.
"I would eat every banana
in the world

just to see her one more time,"
he says, and we both fall
silent, make fists

around the handle
of our grocery cart
and together we push on.

THERE ARE SO MANY CHILDREN

with hearing problems," my father
marvels, as we sink into scratchy
orange seats in the audiologist's

office. He is used to seeing
only *alterkockers* like himself
when he visits the pulmonologist,

cardiologist, retinologist, ophthalmologist
proctologist, dermatologist, endocrinologist
"my friends, the ologists,"

he calls them with a wry smile.
But here, there are children
darting around like fish

being caught by their mothers
and plopped onto laps, only
to wriggle free again. A little boy

sporting a big hearing aid
sprawls on the floor in front
of us piecing together

a jigsaw puzzle. "I did it!"
he crows, throwing his hands
up in the air, before dumping

out the pieces and starting over
again. My father chuckles, hears
himself and stops. "Listen to me

laughing," he mutters in amazement
and disgust. My mother has only
been gone a month and already

he's laughing? "Life goes on,"
I remind my father. He sighs,
and picks up a copy of *Good*

Housekeeping, a magazine
my mother has subscribed to
since 1953; there are issues

scattered all over the house
like tattered takeout menus
from restaurants that closed

long ago. Now my father thumbs
through glossy pages of diets
and recipes, then returns

the magazine to the coffee table
and pushes it away with the tips
of his fingers as if it is too

repulsive to touch. "Your mother
and I had a plan, you know,"
he says. I look up from last

week's *New Yorker.* "What
was it?" I ask, as this is news
to me. "I was supposed to die

first," my father jabs a finger
into the bony hollow above
his heart. "And then your mother

would have taken care
of everything." He sighs
once more and picks up

a copy of *Field and Stream*
which he can't even pretend
to be interested in. *If you want*

to make God laugh, tell God
your plans, my mother told me
at least a hundred times.

Are you happy now? I want
to ask God who really should
have left my mother down here

with me to remind my father
to turn right not left into
the doctor's parking lot,

to push "3" not "4"
in the medical building's
elevator, to help him hand

his driver's license, not his Macy's
charge card to the receptionist,
and to finally drop down

into a seat beside him
to wait and wonder
when on earth he'll be called

MY FATHER IS SLIPPING

his glasses up his nose
eager to see the stars
on TV. "Sure, I'm watching,"

he is quick to assure me.
"Who would want to miss
all the beautiful ladies?"

My father is missing
the beautiful lady
who sat beside him day

after day for over half
a century, gone 6 months
now, her beauty gone

long before that. But my father
thought my mother beautiful
to the very end

and the end was not pretty
to say the least:
my mother down to 100 pounds

her hands curled into claws
her feet bloated as balloons.
But let's forget all that for now

here are the pretty pretty
ladies, pirouetting this way
and that on their needle-

sharp heels, and here's J. Lo
in a gown cut down to here
her breasts like two buttery

biscuits, two luminous moons
two glowing golden globes.
The next day my father

boasts that he stayed up
and upright until the bitter end
as if this is a big deal

which I suppose it is. "The show
was lousy," he says. I wait.
"The host was terrible."

I wait. "The songs were too long."
And? "They picked the wrong movies."
And? "I'm not going to watch it

next year." And? "I sure hope
tomorrow doesn't snow."
For the first time my father

fails to bestow the Best
Breasts of the Evening Award
and that's how I know the ladies'

man my mother loathed
and loved for all her life
has finally slipped away

DID YOU GO TO CITY COLLEGE?

calls an elderly gent in a booth
across the aisle. The Celebrity
Diner is nearly empty, so I imagine

he is talking to us. I glance over and take
in the flannel shirt hanging on his bony
frame, the few wisps of white hair

floating about his head, the brown
age spots dotting his sunken cheeks.
His middle-aged companion who fills

out a similar shirt and looks
a lot like him, locks eyes with me
recognizing a kindred spirit

on the aging parent path,
then shakes his head
in silent apology and turns

his attention back to his phone.
"Dad," I say loudly. My father, digging
into the coleslaw our server set down

along with our menus, ignores me.
"Dad." I tug the sleeve of his suit
jacket. "The man over there is asking

if you went to City College."
My father clanks down his fork.
"How did you know?" he asks

the man who is obviously hungry
for the conversation his son is not
providing. The man points at the class

ring on my father's finger, then holds
up his hand to show off his own.
"What year?" His voice is raspy, hard

for my father to hear. "What year?"
I repeat for my father. "1948," he boasts,
clearly a challenge. "You?"

"1942," the man answers. "I'm 93 years
young," he snickers, clearly proud
at beating my father at his own game.

"I'm 88," says my father, lifting his fork
to stab a pickle, more food brought
by the server before we've even placed

our order. "A mere kid," the man scoffs,
slapping his son lightly on the arm.
The son shrugs—*whatever*—and returns

to studying his phone. My father studies
his own hand. "See this ring?" he asks me.
"I got this ring in 1947. It was too big

so I took it to a jeweler. He told me
the stone was loose and could
fall out any minute. I meant

to replace it but never bothered.
It's still here. And I'm still here."
My father opens his arms wide

presenting himself to the world.
"Maybe I'll get myself a new stone
now. It's not too late, right?"

"Right, Dad," I say. "What do you want
to eat?" I try drawing his attention
back to the atlas-sized menu

in front of him for the third time,
but my father is nowhere
near a decision. "93 years old,"

he glances across the way, nodding.
"And he could see my class ring
all the way from there. That's something."

"Yep," I say. "How about a skirt steak?"
I ask my father who has ordered this
before, joking that he likes anything in a skirt.

My father shrugs—*whatever*—leaving me
to order our food. "Did you ever live…"
my father starts to ask the *landsman*

across the way, then abruptly stops
at the sight of the man's son
fastening a bib around his father's

scrawny neck. Out of respect,
my father turns away to give
the *alterkocker* his privacy, but not

before I see a look of pity and disgust
travel across his face. Our food arrives,
we eat in silence, as does the other

City College alum and his son.
They finish first. The son rises
and offers his arm to his father

who grasps it with both hands,
hoists himself up, then shuffles
forward, stops at our table, nods,

and tips an invisible hat to us.
"You're okay," my father says
to the man who has no idea

that coming from my dad this is high
praise indeed. Father and son
amble toward the door as we finish

eating. And for the first time
I can remember, my father
does not order dessert.

WHO'S THAT?

my father asks, jabbing
his thick yellow nail
at a thin willowy woman

dressed in a beaded evening
gown, staring up at us
from the pages of my parents'

age-old wedding album.
I stare back. "I don't know,
Dad." *Mom would know*

I think, but do not say.
My father squints, adjusts
his cockeyed glasses, brings

the heavy book closer
to his face. "It's you!"
he says, his voice full

of triumph. *See! The old man's
still got a few of his marbles
left!* "That's not me, Dad,"

I say, hating to deflate him.
"No?" The deep creases in his brow
deepen as he lowers the book to his

lap, stares at the photo, stares
at me. "It looks like you,"
he insists, desperate to be right.

"Are you sure it's not you?"
I shake my head. "No, Dad,
it's not me," I repeat, desperate

for him to be in his right mind.
"This is your wedding album. You
got married in 1949. I was born

in 1955." My father scowls.
The numbers do not add up.
"Are you positive?" he asks sadly.

"I'm positive," I answer sadly,
for more than anything I want
to have been there. To have seen

my dreamboat of a dad
in his rented top hat and tails
gazing down at my model-slim mother

in her borrowed veil and lacy gown,
to have heard the rabbi's blessing
and the smash of the glass

beneath my father's foot.
"I wasn't even a twinkle in your eye,"
I say, hoping the old cliché

will make my father smile.
It doesn't. "Who is that?" he asks
again lifting his eyes toward the sky

and rapidly tapping his callused middle
finger against his faded frowning lips.
Who indeed? God only knows

but God isn't saying. "Is it Cousin Irma?"
I ask my father who smacks himself
on the forehead. "What a dummy.

Cousin Irma! Of course that's who
it is," he declares, relieved
to put a name to the face that looks

so much like his clever daughter
who always knows who's who
and what's what, and that desperate

times call for desperate measures,
such as pulling a name—any name!—
out of a hat if it will make the worry

on her father's worrisome face
disappear like magic
as he leans forward

and slowly
but surely
turns another page

HEAVEN CAN RELY ON YOU

sings a chorus of strapping young
men in sweet, deep voices
that blend inside my father's head.

"Don't you hear them?" he asks,
then shrugs, unconcerned about being
the sole witness to this tender serenade.

He holds up a single finger, signaling
wait, wait, the men have stopped
but then they start up again.

"Gouda, gouda, gouda," my father sings along.
"Like the cheese?" I tease, trying
to make light of this newest delusion.

My father frowns—it isn't funny—
and cocks his head, like a puzzled puppy
trying to make sense of what's being said,

the sound—any sound—a precious gift
since he doesn't hear much these days,
not the telephone's startled and startling

shriek, not the blasting TV's blathering
newscaster, not the neighborhood
dog's insistent sharp bark, not the rain's

hard hammer against the sliding glass door,
and not a peep from the little boy
who appears at the foot of his bed

night after night, his eyes as blue
as my father's before the cataracts
floated in, two puffy clouds across

his morning sky. "Who is he, Dad?"
I ask. My father shrugs then lifts
his finger again. "Yes dear,"

he says, "I will, dear." He looks towards
my mother's chair, and out of nowhere
I hear her, too, her voice the weak whisper

of that terrible last day. *Don't worry,
sweetheart.* She cupped my cheek
with her worn, withered hand.

*There's no problem so terrible
that it can't get worse.*
"Gouda gouda gouda,"

sings my father, happily off-key,
swaying in his seat,
his ancient voice cracking

like a young Bar Mitzvah boy's.
Deedle deedle deedle.
Zuzza zuzza zuzza.

THE FIRST TIME WE VISIT

the neurologist, he gives us
exactly 7 minutes of his time.
"What's 8 plus 15?"

he asks my father who gives me
a look I know all too well:
What is this guy, an imbecile?

"8 plus 15 is 23." My father speaks
loudly as if the doctor hears
worse than he does. "C'mon, ask

me a real question." My father puts
up his dukes and punches the air
eager for a good fight.

"8 times 15 is 120.
120 times 15 is 1,800.
1,800 times 15 is 27,000."

The poor neurologist
has no way of knowing what
a math whiz my father is

how he'd entertain us on long car
rides by barking out math problems
or better yet dare me to challenge

him. "Hey Dad, what's 11,327
plus 10,695?" I'd ask.
"22,022," he'd say in a second

waiting for me to work it out
in my notebook. He was always
right. "Hey Dad, what's a million

plus a trillion?" I'd ask, searching
my brain for the biggest number
in the universe. "A million trillion,"

he'd answer. "Hey Dad, what's
a million trillion plus
a million trillion?"

"A ba-a-a-zill-ll-ll-ion,"
he'd say, shaking his head so fast
his cheeks turned to rubber

and I'd crack up. If only
we were laughing now
but the neurologist is not

amused. He leans forward
to study his puzzle of a patient.
"Where were you born?" he asks.

"Brooklyn, naturally,"
my father says as if the doctor
should know that anyone who is

anyone was born in Brooklyn.
"What did you do for a living?"
My father sits up a little taller.

"I'm an attorney. Still practicing."
The neurologist looks to me
to confirm that either this is true

or that my father has gone bananas.
"Yep," I say, hoping to convey
that this is a real problem.

The neurologist does not catch on.
"Who's running for president?" he asks
my father who is now convinced

that the doctor is completely bonkers.
"Hillary and that son of a bitch,"
he bellows, causing the two

receptionists out front to break
into peals of squealing laughter.
"He's fine." The doctor leans back

and glances up at the clock
to let me know I've wasted
enough of his time. "He's great.

Take him home." My father is already
out of his seat. "But what about
his delusions?" I ask, "the men

singing in his head, the little boy
at the foot of his bed?"
The neurologist shrugs.

"Old people have delusions,"
he says, pulling open his file
cabinet's top drawer

clearly done with me
and my father, who is already
out in the waiting room

waving my coat by the shoulders
like a matador taunting a bull
then hustling me down the hallway

C'mon, let's go, shake a leg.
Clearly we have more important things
to do than deal with this nonsense

and this doctor who I know
my father thinks is a real nut job
and will never again agree to see

not next week,
not next month,
not in a bazillion years.

MY FATHER HAS HIS DAY

in court and calls to report
the proceedings. "First
I got in the car and drove

to Brooklyn," he says, though
I have been begging him to take
a cab or car service to work

for weeks. "And you won't believe
what happened," he continues,
my cue to say, "What happened?"

"The parking lot near the courthouse
I've been using for over 50 years
disappeared," says my father, bursting

with the news. "And there's a huge
apartment building there instead.
Must be at least 20 stories high.

Do you believe that?" Of course
I don't believe that. My father,
like me, has a sense of direction

akin to an eggplant. "How did they
build it so fast?" he asks, his voice
rising with wonder. "Dad, maybe you

drove down the wrong street,"
I say, knowing my father,
whom my long-suffering mother

dubbed the U-Turn King of Long Island
will poo-poo this as preposterous.
"Nonsense," he says and then waits

until I ask, "So what did you do?"
so he can go on. "I drove into
Manhattan," he says in a tone that implies

I'm an idiot—*What do you think I did?*
"and parked in a garage I know
near Penn Station on West 33rd.

And then I took the subway
back to Brooklyn. I wasn't
even late," he boasts, proud

of his impeccable punctuality. I sink
onto the kitchen floor, clutching
the phone so tightly my hand cramps

into a claw as I picture my father,
the original Mr. Magoo bumbling
from borough to borough

in his wrongly buttoned London Fog
trench coat, the unbuckled belt
dangling to the ground, his hat

askew, his glasses spotted with rain,
grasping his briefcase with one hand
and hanging from the subway strap

with the other as he sways
around the curves of the crowded
train, too proud to accept the seat

that surely someone must have offered
the bedraggled 89-year-old businessman.
"And guess what happened next?"

asks my father, chomping at the bit
to continue his tale. "What happened
next?" I ask, his scene partner

who knows her lines by heart.
"The security guard let me
into the building without going

through the metal detector.
How do you like that?" My father
speaks with pride as though he himself

has done something remarkable.
"I guess the guy finally
figured out if I haven't blown

the place sky high by now,
I must be okay." Again, I picture
my disheveled father fumbling

to empty his suit pockets
of his heavy collection of keys
most of which lead to nowhere,

his worn out wallet that bulges
like an overstuffed pastrami
on rye from the Second Avenue Deli,

and the antique flip phone he loves
to carry though he has
no clue how to use.

"And you'll never believe this,"
says my father, his voice eager
as the announcer on *The Price*

Is Right – Wait! There's more!
"The judge—I've known her
for 30 years—did something today

she's never done before." He pauses
for dramatic effect. "What?"
I ask, wondering if this saga will

ever end. "She motioned me
to approach the bench and argue
my case right next to her."

Another dramatic pause
followed by a chuckle. "She's
no spring chicken that's for sure.

I think she's going deaf and needed
me near so she could hear."
I know better than to tell my father

that the kindly judge knew
he needed her near so *he* could hear
and say instead, "And then what

happened?" failing to mask
the weariness in my voice.
"Then I took the train back

to Manhattan, found my car,
drove home in rush hour
traffic no less, took me

a good 5 hours. Phew, what a day."
My father finally runs out of steam.
"Dad," I can't help myself.

"Maybe this is all too much for you."
"Nah." My father dismisses me.
"I'm a race horse. I was bred to run."

"But, Dad"—
"Don't start with me."
"But—"

"I mean it." In other words,
he refuses to hear my Closing
Argument, so I hang up and pray

that whoever was watching
over my hellbent father today
will continue to keep

the absentminded attorney
safe and sound
until his trials are over.

MY FATHER DROVE MY MOTHER

crazy for 63 years, one foot on the brake
one foot on the gas, the car lurching
along the Long Island Expressway,

my father steering with his left hand
on the wheel, his right arm slung across
the back of the seat, his hand stroking

my mother's rigid right shoulder
as if it were a frightened feral cat.
Knowing she was taking her life

in her hands by putting her life
in his hands, she sat fuming
in the front seat, chain-smoking

her Chesterfield Kings and saying
not a word as we zigzagged through
rush hour traffic, my father speeding

up, slowing down, switching lanes
all the while singing, "If Ever I Should
Leave You" fancying himself a dead

ringer for a dashing Robert Goulet.
Now she is gone and I am riding
shotgun, buckled in like an anxious child

at an amusement park who has
somehow been convinced to get on
the scariest ride of all. My left hand

grips the edge of the dashboard,
my right foot pumps an invisible
brake and I dare not say a word

to my fearless father lest he turn
away from the road to read my lips
and take us both out once and for all.

As we zoom through a few lights—green,
yellow, red—I narrow my eyes into slits
as if I am watching a horror movie

until I hear a cacophony of beeps and honks
coming from a long row of cars my father
has zipped past before taking a left

from the middle lane, and cutting off
a blue Buick right in front of a police officer
standing on the sidewalk whose head

snaps around as she jumps up and down,
waves her arms frantically and blows
the whistle at my father who murmurs

"Oh shit," as he pulls over and rolls
down his window. The cop looks
young enough to be my daughter

and tough enough to tell my father
what he needs to hear: it's high time
he stopped driving. She peers

into the car and tilts her head at me:
*Really? You let this old guy
behind the wheel?* and asks

for his driver's license. "What the hell
were you thinking, Sir? You ran a red
light and turned from the wrong lane."

My father hangs his head like a naughty
boy, apologizes profusely, promises
to be more careful next time, then roars

with laughter as we roar away, pleased
to get off with only a warning. Back home
he swerves around the corner and clunks

the car—*ka-thunk!*— over the bump at the foot
of the driveway he's been meaning to fix
for 50 years, scrapes the bush

beside the garage door, and races out
of the car towards the house, stopping
only to grab the mail which he rifles

through, tucking a telltale yellow traffic
ticket under his arm. I sit to collect
myself before joining him in the kitchen

for a cup of tea and a conversation
I've waited too long to have but have
rehearsed in my head many times.

Sometimes I pose it as a question:
*Dad, don't you think it's time to stop
driving?* Sometimes I state it as fact:

Dad, it's time for you to stop driving.
Sometimes I appeal to his conscience:
Dad, what if you kill someone? What

if you hurt a child? I steel myself
to start "the talk" but as I set down
our tea, my father speaks first.

"You know," he says, "I had a client
whose kids made him stop driving.
He didn't speak to any of them

for the last 3 years of his life."
He blows on his tea, then takes
a noisy slurp as I let this sink in.

"And you remember Minnie and Abe?
Their oldest son took away the car
keys when Minnie was 95

and Abe was 96. So what did they do?"
My father does not wait for an answer.
"They rented a car twice a week

to get groceries. Where there's a will
there's a way." My father finishes
his tea in one great gulp, pushes

back his chair, stands, and bangs
his mug down on the table
like a gavel: Case Closed.

PAIN IN THE ASS

says my father when his DVD player
refuses to play the tennis tape
he jammed into it. "Pain in the ass,"

says my father when the TV remote
won't change the TV channels.
"Pain in the ass," says my father

when the captions on his captioned
phone disappear. Everything
is a pain in the ass these days:

the dishwasher that leaves a soapy
film on his dishes, the clothes
dryer which won't fully dry his clothes,

his electric toothbrush that won't
turn on, his hearing aids which
whistle an unhappy tune,

the light in the front hallway that
recently burned out, the car radio
that remains stubbornly silent,

even the plastic shoe horn he has
used every day for 40 years
has just this morning cracked

in two. "I don't understand it."
My father throws up his hands
in despair. "Every single thing

I touch turns into disaster.
Look at this." Home early
from work, he flings his brief

case onto the kitchen table,
flips open its two brass clasps,
raises the top, and points

to a disheveled pile of papers
before he even removes his hat
and coat. "What is it?" I lift

the stack of papers to see
if I can straighten them out.
"It's a brief." My father

who has never been known
for his patience tries to wrest
the document out of my hands.

"A very important brief
for a very important case."
I don't point out that every

case is a very important case
to my father, especially now
that he has so few of them.

"Why are there 27 copies
of page one?" I ask, "and
only one copy of the rest?"

My father grabs the document
out of my hands and slaps
it on the table. "I tried

to make copies today
and would you believe that
both copy machines broke down?

Pain in the ass." My father
leafs through the pages as if
he can magically make

them right. "Isn't making copies
your secretary's job?" I ask
my father who is still shuffling

papers around. "She's on vacation,"
he says, his tone implying
she has some nerve, leaving him

to his own devices. "Wasn't there
someone else who could do it?"
I ask, though I know my father

would rather break 100 copiers
than admit he needed help.
"What could they do? I'm telling you

both machines were on the fritz.
Pain in the ass," he repeats, stuffing
the pages back into his briefcase.

"I need to bring these to court
tomorrow. Ach." He slams down
the lid of his briefcase, clicks

the clasps shut, whips it off
the table and hauls it into the den
where he finally removes his hat

and coat and slumps onto the couch.
With a disgruntled sigh, he bends
over and unties his right shoe,

the weak time-worn lace snapping
off in his hand. "Grrrr." He growls
like a cur about to bite

then dangles the broken lace
at a distance between his thumb
and forefinger like it was alive.

"I'll find you a new lace," I say,
as I sink down beside him,
take the lace from his fingers,

and gently lay it on the coffee
table. "Don't bother." My father
kicks off his other shoe

and we sit side by side in silence
staring at his big toe poking through
a good-sized hole in the navy

blue sock on his right foot
which clashes with the forest
green sock on his left. My father

clasps my hand in his and uses it
to pat my knee a few times,
then rests his heavy head

on my shoulder, and reaches
underneath his schmutzy glasses
to wipe his weary eyes.

"What can I tell you, kid?" My father
asks then answers his own question.
"Your old man is falling apart."

THE SECOND TIME WE VISIT

the neurologist, I tell my father
where to go without telling him
where we are going. Once we make

our way inside, I park him in front
of the receptionists so he can flirt
with them while I go in search

of the good doctor. "You've got
to tell him to stop practicing law."
My voice teeters between plea

and demand, a delicate balance.
"And you've got to get him to give
up driving." The neurologist peers

over the rim of his reading glasses,
at someone I am sure he has seen
before: an adult child on the edge

of a nervous breakdown. "Bring him
in," he says and turns his back
while I go fetch my father who is

having a grand old time laughing
with the ladies. "So long, sweetheart."
He whistles the letter "S" and draws

out his words like a film noir star
as I take him by the arm
into the doctor's office and steer

him towards a chair. "Hiya Doc."
My father's good mood continues.
"Got any more math problems for me?"

"Nah," says the neurologist. "You aced
them all last time." The neurologist
flips through a chart on his desk

then whips off his reading glasses.
"You know," he says, "I'm thinking
of giving all this up." He waves a hand

about the room. "It's no fun anymore.
It's all about the goddamn insurance.
I'm thinking I might go into law."

"Really?" asks my father. *Really?*
I wonder where he's going
with this. Maybe the neurologist

is a nut job as my father suspects.
"I'm looking into law schools,"
he continues. "Got any advice

for me?" My father straightens up
and sits still to collect his thoughts,
thrilled to be in his element. He points

one finger to the ceiling and says,
"The law is a jealous mistress,"
then pauses to let that sink in.

"That's the first thing my first law
professor told me on the first day
of class." As my father sits back,

my parents' entire marriage
flashes before my eyes:
my father leaving for work early

in the morning before the sky grew
light, returning in the evening
after the sky grew dark, warming

his dinner in the toaster oven
then eating alone, yellow legal
pads strewn across the table,

Saturdays spent at the office,
Sundays spent on the phone with
crazy clients, my mother puffing

away on her cigarettes, fury
and smoke mingling in the air.
"So how's work going for you?"

the neurologist leans forward to ask.
"Meh." My father holds out one hand
and flips it over several times.

"Comme ci comme ça. I'm not
as young as I used to be. Plus
my hearing's not all that great."

My father blows out a long
breath, as if finally admitting this
has lifted a great weight.

"Maybe it's time for you to give
it up," the neurologist says gently.
"Maybe." My father thinks it over.

"I suppose you're right." He collapses
back against his seat and drops
his head into his hands, his face

so full of defeat I have to turn
away. "And how's your driving?"
asks the neurologist who has no

qualms about punching a man when
he's down. My father presses his lips
together and I fear he might cry.

"Not so good at night. Cataracts."
He shrugs and the neurologist nods.
"I think you need to give that up

too." My father blinks a few times
and heaves another sigh. "Okay
dokey," he says, and now I stare

openly, wondering who is this beaten
man who has taken over my father's
body? He pushes himself to his feet

extends his right hand and says
"Good luck, Doc. Study hard."
The neurologist takes my father's

hand in both his own and meets
his eye. "Good luck to you too,
sir." Then there is nothing

left to say, so we make our way
back through the waiting room
my father not even stopping

to bid farewell to the receptionists
who perk up at the sight of him.
In the elevator, he fishes

his car keys out of his pocket
and dangles them in front of me.
We emerge from the building

squinting into bright sunlight,
like coming out of a dark
movie theatre in the middle

of the day. I slide behind the wheel,
adjust the seat and mirrors, wait
for my father to buckle up.

The last time we sat side by side
like this was more than 40 years
ago when he taught me how

to drive, yanking the braid that fell
halfway down my back, yelling,
"Whoa Nellie!" when we got

to a red light, and crying, "Giddy-up!"
the second it turned green.
Now my father stares straight

ahead without speaking, and
as I pull into traffic, I remember
a time I really wanted something—

a new toy, a new dress, a new puppy—
something my parents wouldn't
allow, and my mother saying

the second saddest thing
in the world is not getting
what you want. I thought

about that and asked her
what's the first saddest thing?
She looked at me with pity.

Getting what you want, she replied.
I never knew what she meant
by that, but now at last I do.

IT WAS

not a stroke
of genius
it was not

a stroke
of luck
it was

a stroke
of misfortune
that befell

my father
leaving him
crumpled

at the foot
of the driveway
next to the garbage

waiting
all morning
to be picked up

MY HANDSOME ELEGANT FATHER

in his freshly pressed grey wool suit
starched white shirt (easy on the collar)
and cranberry juice-colored tie

wearing the cufflinks shaped like subway
tokens I bought him for his birthday
and spit shiny black Italian leather shoes

freshly showered
cleanly shaven
fingernails carefully clipped and buffed

smelling of Ivory Soap,
Old Spice, Brylcreme,
Listerine, and Arid Extra Dry

holding his monogrammed leather
briefcase by the handle, off to work
at 8:00 in the morning

returning at 7:00 in the evening
6 days a week,
4 weeks a month

12 months a year
for more than half a century
my handsome elegant father

now dragging an IV pole
through the hospital hallway
barefoot, grizzly-chinned

hair like Albert Einstein
sweaty and stinky
wearing a sky blue johnny

dotted with tiny tumbling teddy
bears, the back flapping open
every string untied

IS THAT ANGUS?

asks my father, sitting up
and pointing to the Saint
Bernard wearing a polka dotted bow

tie and vest that matches those
of the therapist strolling
into the ICU where my father

lies waiting to see if he needs
surgery on his corroded
carotid artery. "No Dad,"

I say as he strokes
the soft fur of the dog
that in no way resembles

Angus, the wiry Toto
look-alike we owned
50 years ago. "How

was lunch?" I ask my father
who frowns and points to his ear
the universal signal for *I can't hear you.*

"HOW WAS LUNCH?" I yell
and then point to my own ear.
"WHERE ARE YOUR HEARING

AIDS?" He shrugs like he doesn't
know and doesn't care. This is not
like my father who cares

plenty since those hearing aids
cost him over three grand
a piece. I search his room

while his blood knocks
on the locked door
of the blockage that stands

guard to his brain. *Look*
for the silver lining, my mother
always said, always an impossible

task especially today, until I realize
that the man behind the curtain
in the cubicle next to my father

and whom we both know
has the exact same condition
is receiving his last rites

from a Father who
thank God my father
can't begin to hear

WHAT TOOK YOU SO LONG?

asks my father, the deep lines
of his forehead deepening
with worry. He pushes himself

up in his hospital bed, reaches
out both pale skinny arms
and opens and shuts his hands

as fast as he can like a child
eager for a long-awaited birthday
present. If I didn't know better

I'd think he was beckoning me
to run to his side for a tender
father/daughter hug, but what

he really wants are the morning papers
I knew better than to arrive without.
I hand over *Newsday,* the *Wall Street*

Journal and *The New York Times*
and watch my father fling open
the *Times* Business Section like a door

to a meeting he was afraid he'd miss
and then disappear completely behind
the newsprint. As he scans the headlines

I scan his room: plate of soggy
scrambled eggs and dry white
toast untouched beside his bed,

dirty crumpled tissues scattered
across his crinkled sheets, TV remote
and emergency call button dangling

by their cords down to the linoleum
floor. I move my father's bare scaly feet
his thick yellow toenails badly in need

of cutting and plop down beside them.
My father lowers the paper
and I joke, "Any good news today?"

but he ignores my question.
"How are you, Dad?" I ask. He answers
"Fine," and then repeats himself,

"Fine," as if first he has to convince
me and then he has to convince himself.
"I'm fine," he states again. "How else

would I be? I'm surrounded by beautiful
women, what's bad?" He gestures
towards a no-nonsense nurse bustling

about the room. "Thank you, darling,"
he says as she hands him a colorful
collection of pills. *"L'chiam."* He raises

a cup of murky-looking cold coffee
high above his head, shakes his fist
full of pills like he's playing craps

then pours his meds into his mouth
snaps his head back and swallows
like a pro. "You'll never guess

who came to see me last night."
My father waits for me to guess
but I haven't a clue. "Joe!"

he cries with utter delight.
"Joe, can you believe it? I look
up and there's Joe, big as life

standing right there by the door.
How do you like that?" I glance
towards the doorway as if Joe

might still be standing there.
"Joe who?" I ask, looking back
at my father who frowns and darts

his eyes back and forth as he runs
through the Rolodex inside his head.
"You know. Joe what's-his-name."

"Oh, Joe Schmoe," I try to kid
away my father's frustration
but when he answers with a grunt

I start in with the twenty questions:
"Joe from the office?
Joe from the club?

Joe from the neighborhood?"
My father waves his hand to
shoo away my nonsense. "Joe,"

he insists. "Joe Weinberg, Joe Weinstein. . . .
Oh c'mon." He knocks the side
of his head with the heel of his hand

trying to shake Joe's last name loose.
"Joe Wisenheimer?" I ask, being
a bit of a Wisenheimer myself.

"Joe Oppenheimer!" My father crows
in triumph. "He has some nerve
showing up here like that after

all this time without a word, a note,
a phone call, nothing. That Joe.
Still owes me a grand and a half

from 50 years ago. He was one
of my first clients. Joe Oppenheimer,"
my father marvels. "What I don't

understand is how he knew I was
in here. Did you tell him?" My father
points an accusing finger.

"No Dad. I didn't tell him. I don't
even know him." My father curls
his lip and shakes his head

with disapproval, as if my not
knowing Joe Oppenheimer is
a grave mistake. Then he brightens.

"Gentlemen! Come in!" My father
bows in his bed and extends his arm
as though he is welcoming guests

to a formal dinner party. I glance over
my shoulder to see Larry and Stu,
two lawyers from my father's building

filling the doorway. "You'll never guess
who came to see me last night."
My father waits only a split second

before blurting, "Joe Oppenheimer!"
Larry and Stu exchange looks.
"Joe Oppenheimer?" Larry asks.

"Joe Oppenheimer," my father answers.
"Joe Oppenheimer?" Stu repeats.
"Joe Oppenheimer," I confirm.

"Are you sure?" Larry asks my father.
"Sure," he replies. "He was standing
right there." He points past us

and both men turn around and then
turn back. "That's impossible," Stu says
to my father. "Joe Oppenhemier

died over 30 years ago."
Larry and Stu look stunned
but I am not the least bit

surprised to learn that of all
the people my father could
have conjured up

my dead mother
his dead mother
his dead father

his dead sister
his dead brother
he chose Joe

some bastard who still owes
him fifteen-hundred bucks
from almost a lifetime ago.

WITHOUT WARNING MY FATHER

is sprung from the hospital early Friday
evening, seeming no better yet no worse
according to the doctor who dismisses

him with an indifferent wave of his hand
a little too eager to get on with his weekend
plans. My father refuses my offer of help

and gets dressed in slow motion, then insists
that I pack up a week's worth of newspapers,
a half-empty box of tissues, a flimsy comb,

a toothbrush, and a kidney-shaped pink plastic
spittoon. Satisfied that he is leaving nothing
behind, he smiles and waves like royalty

as an aide pushes him past the nurse's station
down the long hallway, into the groaning
elevator and out to the parking lot.

It's not until we drive halfway home and stop
at a red light where a family of five crosses
the street—father in gray suit with white sneakers

gleaming on his feet, mother in long dark skirt,
daughters all dolled up, subdued and somber—
that I realize it's Yom Kippur, the Holiest

Day of the year. *"Gut yontif,"*
I say to my father, pointing. He stares
but does not wish me a good holiday

in return. When we arrive home, he heads
straight for the den and instantly falls
asleep, a lazy boy in his La-Z-Boy,

hands clasped on chest, thumbs twitching
through his dreams. Darkness falls
an hour later and he startles awake,

looks around as if he has no idea
where he is, sees me, sighs, says
"God will forgive us," and dozes off

again. I tuck a green and black afghan
my mother knit 100 years ago
under his chin, as I remember sitting

in synagogue with my father when I was
a little girl. How I loved braiding the *tzit-tzit*
of his *tallis,* the white fringe so smooth

and cool beneath my fingers, while the men
all around me swayed and prayed, their deep
voices wringing as much sweetness

and sadness out of those ancient words
as they could, that heartrending Hebrew
comforting me like a soft shawl wrapped

around my small slender shoulders.
I stood when my father stood,
bowed my head when my father

bowed his head, sat when my father sat,
his "Amen" the sweetest and saddest
of all. Last year for the first time,

we drove to services, my father unable
to manage the two-mile walk between home
and *shul.* We sat up front hoping that would

help him hear, but after the third time
he asked, "What page? What page?"
licking his finger and frantically flipping

through the prayer book like he was
looking for an important number
in an outdated phone book,

I was relieved when his head dropped
to his chin, then mortified once more
when he began to snore so loudly

the rabbi threw me a look and I took
my father home. I know God will
forgive my poor aged and aging

father for not attending temple
on this Day of Atonement
but I don't know if the same God

will forgive me for not knowing
what's best: to pray or not to pray
for the Book of Life to be inscribed

at the start of the new year
with my father's holy name
underneath my own

FOR AS LONG AS I CAN

remember my father has been
a creature of habit. Every morning
he rose at exactly 6:00 a.m.—

no need to set the clock—
jumped into the shower, shaved,
slapped his cheeks with cologne,

donned a suit and tie, thudded
down the stairs, punched in
the code to shut the burglar

alarm, yanked open the front door,
hustled down the driveway,
fetched the newspapers,

clamored into the kitchen,
sat at the head of the table,
poured out a bowl of Special K,

added 2% milk, filled his "World's
Greatest Dad" mug with Instant
Maxwell House laced with Sweet

'N Low, skimmed the headlines
of *Newsday* and the *Times,*
gobbled up his cereal, gulped down

his coffee, clattered his dirty dishes
into the sink, threw on his overcoat,
grabbed his leather briefcase,

dashed out of the house,
punched in the code
to re-set the burglar alarm,

locked the front door,
unlocked his Nissan Maxima,
started her up, backed out,

and sped to the office,
arriving before anyone else
at exactly 7:45. My father

thought this routine would last
forever—why wouldn't it?—
and cannot for the life of him

fathom how quickly he went
from husband to widower
attorney to retiree

tennis partner to spectator
driver to passenger
healthy to diabetic

hearing to practically deaf
seeing to practically blind
and if all that wasn't bad

enough now his beloved
daughter—of all people!—
is trying to convince him

to go from lifelong New Yorker
to new New Jersey-ite,
from proud homeowner

to reluctant resident
of what might as well be
called God's Waiting Room.

"I don't like it." My father
puckers up his face and whines
like a little boy who has just been

presented with a plate of liver
and lima beans, instead of
a colorful brochure exalting

the perks of downsizing,
the benefits of independent living
and the joys of communal life.

I don't like it either—
this hurts me more
than it hurts you

floats through my mind—
but before I can stop myself
I make the calls,

send for the paperwork,
and lower the shades
of the living room window

so my father doesn't have
to see the green For Sale sign
blooming on his lawn

MY FATHER IS MOVING OUT

of the house he shared with my mother
for more than 50 years and every damn
day I find a brand new way to break

his broken heart. "Dad." I place
a plate of French toast with sugar-
free syrup in front of him to sweeten

this morning's bitter pill. "I'm going
to clean out Mom's closet today."
My father lowers the Sports section

of *The New York Times* and scrapes
back his chair. "I'll do it," he says,
dashing up the stairs before

I can down my last slurp of coffee.
"Wait for me," I yell as if he were
a child about to step into traffic

then race upstairs to find him
standing in my mother's musty, dusty
boudoir, staring at her closet

door which hasn't been opened once
in the last 4 years. "Dad, maybe
you should let me do this," I say

but he doesn't move, so I reach
past him and swing the door wide.
Instantly we are assaulted by her smell,

a mixture of Chesterfield Kings,
Noxzema, Aqua Net, and
Chanel No. 5 still clinging to a lifetime

of dresses, blouses, skirts, shirts,
slacks, slips, shoes, scarves, gloves,
hats, pocketbooks and pantyhose.

My father staggers backwards, catching
himself in the doorjamb, and when I pull
out the first item—a polyester leopard

print number my mother wore when
she waltzed into the surprise party
my father threw for her 65th birthday—

the look of shock on his face shatters
my shattered heart. It's as if he is just
now realizing that she is gone

for good. "Dad," I take him by the arm.
"Why don't you go downstairs?
The Yankees are playing." I blast the TV

and set him up with a jar of Planters
peanuts and a can of Diet Coke, then
drag myself back to the task at hand.

Where to begin? I gaze at stripes, plaids,
polka dots, paisleys, lace, sequins, and
sparkles. I run my hands along silk, velvet,

velour, cotton, leather, suede and wool.
I make my way to the back of the closet
and come face to face with 5 hanging

shoe bags, each one with 16 pockets.
80 pairs of size 6 shoes, all once
slipped onto my mother's dainty feet:

The pink silk pumps dyed to match
the evening gown she wore to her eldest
nephew's Bar Mitzvah in 1952.

The gold lamé, kitten-heeled flip-flops
she wore to the beauty parlor for her
monthly pedicures. The beloved pair of red

patent leather stilettos that showed
off her shapely calves. And the despised
boxy navy blue sneakers she had

to wear after the cancer bloated
her feet into Cinderella step-sister
monstrosities. I toss shoe after shoe

after shoe into cardboard boxes,
thud thud thud like the clumps of dirt
we dumped on top of her plain pine coffin

such a long and short time ago.
Afternoon melts into evening,
the Yankees lose, and the clothes

that still hold my mother's DNA fill
50 bags that fill the living room.
The next morning I lug everything outside

to wait for Big Brothers/Big Sisters
to haul it all away. At exactly 6:30
my father emerges to fetch

the morning papers, sees me,
and halts as his right hand flies
up to shield his eyes from the sun

as if he is saluting the rows of clothes
that line the driveway from garage
to curb. Together we stand guard

over my mother's garments
until a driver pulls up his truck
and chucks everything into the back.

My father signs on the dotted line
and pockets the tax receipt he is given.
It takes all of 5 minutes

and then the truck disappears
and I lead my father back inside
the house which is no longer a home.

IT TAKES A LONG TIME

to die," says my father
who is sick
and tired of everyone

telling him how great.
he looks. He is almost
90 with a full head

of hair and a full set
of teeth and he has kept
his "girlish figure"

of which he has always
been immensely proud.
"Everyone says I look

like I'm 60," he gloats.
"Dad, I'm 60," I remind him.
He scrunches up his nose

shakes his head and flicks
his fingers twice, dismissing
my words which can't

possibly be true. How can
he be old enough to have
a 60-year-old daughter?

"The women are beating
down my door," he brags,
before rousing himself

off his rocker
to gather a fistful
of notes strewn

about the living room.
He fans them across
his cluttered coffee table.

Pick a card any card
I think, as I read
invitations from Doris

Sylvia, Gladys, Marlene
asking him to play Bingo,
Scrabble, Monopoly, Risk.

"Dear Mr. N,"
"Howdy New Neighbor!"
"From One New Yorker

To Another."
In pristine printing
scribbled script

pen, pencil, even pink ink
the ladies invite
my fetching father

to take a walk
watch a film
share a meal

drink some tea.
"So what do you think?"
I ask him neatly

stacking the notes
into a pile on the table
next to a teetering tower

of junk mail asking
my father for money
beside a mountain of unread

law journals and other magazines.
My father flicks his fingers
again and gives a little snort

as if he can't be bothered.
"The thought of being
with a woman

other than your mother
is repulsive to me,"
he says stiffly

as though he has rehearsed
it. "So can I throw these
away?" I ask, always eager

to straighten up his new apartment,
a Sisyphean task. "Leave them,"
says my father, the original pack

rat who has stashed beneath
his bed several shoe
boxes of birthday cards

and anniversary cards
collected over 60-plus years,
each one signed by my mother

always and forever.
"Why do you want them?"
I ask my father who shrugs,

his new answer to everything.
"I'll take care of them
later," he promises

which we both know means
they will remain right here
where I drop them

on his coffee table
next to a cigar box
full of family photos

an empty bottle of baby aspirin
a cup of tea grown cold
always and forever

THE PEOPLE NEXT DOOR

fight every night," says my father,
his raspy voice rising on the phone.
"They yell, they scream, they

carry on, You bitch! You bastard!
They slap each other, they punch
each other, they kick each other,

He's beating me! She's beating me!
night after night after night,
I'm telling you, no one can do

anything, even the cops can't make them
stop. I don't know how they allow it.
I haven't had a decent night's

sleep since I moved in here.
I've never heard anything like it.
I swear I'm losing my mind."

"Dad, I'm very sorry to hear this," I say.
"Dad, that sounds very unpleasant," I say.
"Dad, don't worry, I'll speak to them," I say

because I am the daughter
who takes care of everything.
I am the daughter

who fixes everything.
I am the daughter who doesn't
have the heart

to tell her disturbed
and disturbing father
there are no people next door.

DID YOU HAPPEN TO SPEAK

to your agent today?" is the new
way my father begins each of our
phone calls. This is because I have

trained him not to say, "Did you
get a check in the mail today?"
which was after I intsructed him

to stop asking, "Did you bring home
any bacon this week?"
My father speaks the language

of money: *shekels,* sawbucks,
dinero, dough. He worked
his whole life: on his knees

shining shoes in Penn Station,
hawking newspapers till he was
hoarse on 42nd Street, selling ice

cream sandwiches to the sunbathers
of Brighton Beach, the heavy tray's
strap digging into the back

of his neck, the hot sand burning
his bare, blistering feet.
My father worked his way

through City College and Brooklyn Law
becoming a big hot shot
attorney so my mother wouldn't want

for anything. Nothing made him
happier than wheeling and dealing
except getting the check

and running through the front
door, dashing into the TV room,
depositing a big fat

kiss on my mother's offered
left cheek, and dropping
a big fat check into her

upturned right hand.
He'd step back and stand
before her, fidgeting

like the school boy
in knickers he once was
eager for his mother

to praise the "A" he received
on his latest spelling test.
My mother would study the check,

say, "Very good, dear,"
then fold it into the deep
pocket of her housecoat

and return to *Wheel of Fortune,*
Jeopardy, or the six o'clock news.
He made the money, she spent it.

That was their deal and it worked
for 63 years.
Then she died and there was no

one to bring home the bacon to
so what was the point? Now
he receives the same piddly

social security check
month after month after month
boring as the tasteless

meals they dish up
day after day after day
in the dull dining room

he is forced to eat in
night after night after night
everything he's ever worked for

amounting to nothing
but this one lousy
done deal

I WISH MY FATHER

a very happy birthday
and yell in his ear, "Dad,
can you believe you're 90?"

He backs out of my hug,
tilts his head to one side
and peers at me intently

trying to figure out
if what I'm saying is true.
Then he collapses

onto a kitchen chair
as if the weight
of every day

of those 90 years
is pressing down
on him hard.

"Got any words
of wisdom, Dad?"
I try to lighten the mood.

He sighs, deeply,
shakes his head vigorously
and then begins to speak.

"My mother died at 80,
my brother at 50,
my sister at 35.

I don't know when my father
died. Maybe he never did.
He'd be 127 now, the old bastard

and it would serve him right.
I haven't seen him since 1939
when he went out for a pack

of cigarettes and never came back.
I was 12 and went right to work
shining shoes for a penny

selling newspapers for a nickel.
Later I went to CCNY and became a CPA.
I was always a numbers man

but never thought I'd make it
to 90. In my day no one lived
to be 90. Who would want to?

Certainly not me, but here I am
blood pressure 120/80, pulse 60
all 32 teeth still in my mouth

How did I get to be so unlucky?
I was supposed to drop dead
at my desk when I was 75

maybe 80, and leave your mother
a million bucks.
Who knew her days

were numbered? 4 score,
4 years more and then
poof! abracadabra

she was gone.
That was some lousy trick
her disappearing act.

How could she leave me
to my lonesome
to carry on without her

for 4 years
8 months
3 weeks

6 days…"
he looks at his watch,
"19 hours,

27 minutes,
and 32 seconds,
but hey," he shrugs, "who's counting?"

BEFORE HE WAS A HUSBAND,

a father, a grandfather,
a great-grandfather, he tells me
he was a "handsome young lad"

with "barely two nickels to rub
together," which was just enough
to take the girl of his dreams

out on a Saturday night. The subway
rumbled into the station as she sat
while he hung from a strap

until they reached Whitehall Terminal
and got off to get on the Staten Island Ferry.
It was a moonless star-studded night.

The sea sloshed against the stern.
They stood side by side
watching Manhattan's skyline

disappear, her head anchored on his shoulder
his arm tied around her waist.
He knew he had exactly 25 minutes

to steal a kiss before they reached the shore.
He asked Lady Liberty to wish him luck
as he gathered his girl into the safe harbor

of his arms and leaned towards her.
The two of them drifted away
until they reached the end of the line . . .

That was 70 years ago.
Now he is 90.
Now she is gone.

Now he has 3 children,
4 grandchildren,
2 great-grandchildren.

Now he has diabetes,
high blood pressure,
a pacemaker.

Now he doesn't know
if it's Sunday or Monday,
if he takes two yellow pills

and one white pill each morning
or the other way around,
if he already read the newspaper

this morning or not and why it matters,
the news is all bad anyway.
He'd rather close his eyes

take a little rest and remember
the gentle weight of her head on his shoulder,
the sweet curve of her waist under his hand,

the softness of her lips against his,
the stars shining, the sea sloshing,
what a gift to drift away…

ON THE DAY WE DISCUSSED

my father giving up
his practice, selling his house,
and moving to independent living,

we sat at the kitchen table
and I shouted, not too loudly
but loudly enough for him to hear

the questions he didn't want
to hear. I couldn't blame him
for turning away from me

without a word
looking left, then right
then fixing his gaze

on a stubborn spot
of spaghetti sauce
above the stove

squinting his faded blue eyes
as he tried to envision
an impossible future

or perhaps finally reading
the writing on the wall.
I watched as he rapidly

tapped the thick yellow nail
of the callused middle finger
of his left hand against

his jutting lower lip
like he always did when he
knew he'd gotten himself

into a jam he couldn't get
out of. After a long time
he heaved a sigh of sorrow

shrugged his shrunken shoulders
and shook his heavy head.
"All right." He held up his hands

in a gesture of surrender
saying what I wanted
and didn't want to hear.

"I'll give it a year," he said
as if he was doing me a favor.
And then what? I hadn't asked

as I swung into action,
making a thousand calls
writing a hundred checks

doing all that needed to be done
so that he could retire,
sell the house, and move.

He lasted exactly 11 months
and 27 days.
Always a man of his word.

MY FATHER WAS NEVER

on time once in his entire life.
We could always count
on him being a good 20 minutes

early. I remember many a Saturday
night with my father dressed
to the nines in his sleek black tux

and glittering diamond studs
pacing the hallway from front
door to kitchen to dining room

before ordering me to dash
upstairs and see what was taking
my impossible mother so goddamn

long. I'd find her sitting side saddle
on a stool in a white silk slip
surrounded by crumpled tissues

imprinted with lip prints
of lipstick the color of apples,
clasping a sparkling bracelet

around her wrist, clipping
on a pair of matching earrings
and muttering to herself in the bedroom

mirror. "I know the early bird catches
the worm. But who the hell
wants a goddamn worm?" She'd hand

me a pendant shaped like a tear
to fasten around her neck,
then raise a silver aerosol can

the hairspray hissing like a snake
as she circled her head 3 times
forcing me to step back from the cloud

that always made me cough. Once
I came home from college
for Thanksgiving and my father

drove me to the airport for my return
flight on a snowy Sunday afternoon.
Somehow my stuffed-to-the-gills suitcase

never made it out to the car.
After he finished yelling and screaming
and carrying on, my father drove

us home and drove us back
to the airport and I was still
an hour early for my flight.

It made me laugh when my father
proudly showed me a note
he received after my mother died:

Dear Mr. Newman,
Thank you for coming to my Bar Mitzvah.
You were the first one there.

I wonder just how early he was
and how on earth he would feel
to learn that from this day forth

for all time he will always
and forever be known
as the late Mr. Newman.

MY MOTHER IS AT THE BRIDGE

table with Loretta, Gert
and Pearl, when my father
finds his way to Heaven.

"Sit down, dear," she says,
patting the seat beside her
and barely looking up from the hand

she's been dealt. "The game is
almost through." But my father is
too overcome to sit. He stands

and stares at his beloved, free
of wheelchair and oxygen tank
happily puffing away

on a Chesterfield King
held between two perfectly
manicured fingers, sipping

a cup of Instant Maxwell
House, leaving a bright red
lip print on the white china cup

her hair the lovely chestnut brown
it was the day they met,
her face free of worry

lines, the diamond pendant
he bought her on their first trip
to Europe glittering

against her ivory throat.
She looks like the star
of an old black-and-white movie

who would never give him
the time of day but somehow
spent 63 years by his side.

"I missed you," my father
tells my mother, leaning down
to kiss her offered cheek.

"Of course you did,"
says my mother, who always
knows everything.

She plays her cards
right, and after Loretta and Pearl
and Gert fold, she stands to let

my father take her in his arms
and in their heavenly bodies
they dance.

Acknowledgments

"The First Time We Visit" was selected by Marie Howe for Honorable Mention in the 2020 Robinson Jeffers Tor House Prize for Poetry, and appears in the Tor House Foundation Newsletter and website.

"My Mother Is At The Bridge" was selected for Honorable Mention in the 2020 Allen Ginsberg Poetry Awards and appears in the *Paterson Literary Review,* issue #49, Spring 2021.

The author offers heartfelt thanks and endless appreciation to Headmistresses Mary Meriam and Risa Denenberg whose support of my poetry means the world to me; my extraordinary agent Elizabeth Harding and her two wonderful assistants, Sarah Gerton and Jazmia Young; the amazingly talented artist Carol Marine whose gorgeous paintings grace the cover of all three of my Headmistress poetry collections; first readers Ellen LaFlèche and Richard Michelson, two of the most gifted poets I know; writing group members Ann Turner, Barbara Diamond Goldin, Corinne Demas, Ellen Wittlinger, Jane Yolen, and Patricia MacLachlan whose feedback and love is invaluable; many many friends and family members who were there when I needed them, and of course Mary Newman Vazquez who makes all things possible.

About the Author

Lesléa Newman has created 75 books for readers of all ages including the poetry collections *I Carry My Mother* which was named a 2016 "Must Read" title by the Massachusetts Center for the Book and received the 2016 Golden Crown Literary Society Poetry Award, and *October Mourning: A Song for Matthew Shepard* which received the 2013 American Library Association Stonewall Honor and the 2014 Florida Council of Teachers of English Joan F. Kaywell Books Save Lives Award. Other titles include the children's books *Gittel's Journey: An Ellis Island Story* (2019 National Jewish Book Award), *Ketzel, The Cat Who Composed* (2016 Massachusetts Book Award and Sydney Taylor Award) and the children's classic, *Heather Has Two Mommies.* Her literary prizes include poetry fellowships from the National Endowment for the Arts and the Massachusetts Artists Foundation. Nine of her books have been Lambda Literary Award finalists. From 2008 -2010, she served as the poet laureate of Northampton, MA. Currently she is a faculty member of Spalding University's School of Creative and Professional Writing program.

Headmistress Press Books

Demoted Planet - Katherine Fallon

Earlier Households - Bonnie J. Morris

The Things We Bring with Us: Travel Poems - S.G. Huerta

The Water Between Us - Gillian Ebersole

Discomfort - Sarah Caulfield

The History of a Voice - Jessica Jopp

I Wish My Father - Lesléa Newman

Tender Age - Luiza Flynn-Goodlett

Low-water's Edge - Jean A. Kingsley

Routine Bloodwork - Colleen McKee

Queer Hagiographies - Audra Puchalski

Why I Never Finished My Dissertation - Laura Foley

The Princess of Pain - Carolyn Gage & Sudie Rakusin

Seed - Janice Gould

Riding with Anne Sexton - Jen Rouse

Spoiled Meat - Nicole Santalucia

Cake - Jen Rouse

The Salt and the Song - Virginia Petrucci

mad girl's crush tweet - summer jade leavitt

Saturn coming out of its Retrograde - Briana Roldan

i am this girl - gina marie bernard

Week/End - Sarah Duncan

My Girl's Green Jacket - Mary Meriam

Nuts in Nutland - Mary Meriam & Hannah Barrett

Lovely - Lesléa Newman

Teeth & Teeth - Robin Reagler

How Distant the City - Freesia McKee

Shopgirls - Marissa Higgins

Riddle - Diane Fortney

When She Woke She Was an Open Field - Hilary Brown

A Crown of Violets - Renée Vivien tr. Samantha Pious

Fireworks in the Graveyard - Joy Ladin

Social Dance - Carolyn Boll

The Force of Gratitude - Janice Gould

Spine - Sarah Caulfield

I Wore the Only Garden I've Ever Grown - Kathryn Leland

Diatribe from the Library - Farrell Greenwald Brenner

Blind Girl Grunt - Constance Merritt

Acid and Tender - Jen Rouse

Beautiful Machinery - Wendy DeGroat

Odd Mercy - Gail Thomas

The Great Scissor Hunt - Jessica K. Hylton

A Bracelet of Honeybees - Lynn Strongin

Whirlwind @ Lesbos - Risa Denenberg

The Body's Alphabet - Ann Tweedy

First name Barbie last name Doll - Maureen Bocka

Heaven to Me - Abe Louise Young

Sticky - Carter Steinmann

Tiger Laughs When You Push - Ruth Lehrer

Night Ringing - Laura Foley

Paper Cranes - Dinah Dietrich

On Loving a Saudi Girl - Carina Yun

The Burn Poems - Lynn Strongin

I Carry My Mother - Lesléa Newman

Distant Music - Joan Annsfire

The Awful Suicidal Swans - Flower Conroy

Joy Street - Laura Foley

Chiaroscuro Kisses - G.L. Morrison

The Lillian Trilogy - Mary Meriam

Lady of the Moon - Amy Lowell, Lillian Faderman, Mary Meriam

Irresistible Sonnets - ed. Mary Meriam

Lavender Review - ed. Mary Meriam